Tarantula Spiders as Pets

The Ultimate Tarantula Owner's Guide

Tarantula breeding, where to buy, types, care, temperament, cost, health, handling, diet, and much more included!

By: Lolly Brown

Foreword

Among exotic pets, the tarantula is fast gaining popularity among keepers and hobbyists. Of course, there are many individuals who might never grow fond of these hairy spiders, but for others, there is a true fascination, admiration and respect for these wonderful and fascinating creatures.

If you have ever thought of keeping a tarantula as a pet but had no idea where to begin, this book brings together much of current knowledge regarding tarantula husbandry. Of course, there is much that is still unknown about this strange spider, but as many keepers and hobbyists will tell you, much of your knowledge will come as much from learning, study, asking questions, observation, and practical experience.

Table of Contents

Introduction

Keeping any pet entails responsibilities, but none more so than for a potentially dangerous arachnid such as a tarantula. And it isn't just the potential danger they could pose to yourself and the people in your household, but it also means the care and responsibility required to keep one of these amazing creatures not just surviving, but thriving.

As the number of tarantula pets have increased in recent years, so have the availability of captive bred tarantulas that are available in the market. This means that tarantulas are easier than ever to come by. But the ease of buying them does not mean that it is something you can simply do on a whim. Tarantulas can potentially live for years – sometimes 20 or more years – which means that keeping one as a pet entails your own dedication to their care for that long.

Feeding them live prey, keeping their cage clean, and making sure that they are free of illnesses and diseases – and doing this for several years requires dedication, commitment, and of course, money. And throughout that time, they might never show you an ounce of affection. But there are rewards to being able to care for such an animal – watching it grow, mature, and live out their lives in relative contentment. If you approach tarantula keeping with the right mindset, it can be one of the most satisfying tasks you can take on.

Glossary of Tarantula Terms

Arachnid – arthropods with four pairs of legs and one pair of pedipalps

Arboreal – lives off the ground

Book lungs – little flaps underneath the abdomen which the tarantula uses to breathe

Carapace – hardened, top half of the shell

CB – Captive Bred

Chelicera – the spider's fangs

Epigastric furrow – the pocket where the male sperm is stored in the female

Exoskeleton – thick shell of an invertebrate

Gravid – pregnant with eggs

Instar – the number of molts that a tarantula has gone through

Invertebrate – no spine, and no internal skeleton; these usually have an exoskeleton

Molt – shedding of the old exoskeleton in order to grow

New World – tarantulas from the Americas

Old world – tarantulas that come from Asia, Africa, and Europe

Opisthosoma – the abdomen

Oviparous – egg-laying

Pedipalp – leg-like appendages on the front of a tarantula, used by males to hold the sperm during mating

Prosoma – front segment, or "head" of the spider

Sling – spiderling; baby spider

Spinnerents – rear appendages used to spin webbing

Substrate – substance used to line the floor of a terrarium

Terrestrial – lives on the gorund

Tibial spurs – hooks on the front pair of legs and used by the males to secure the female's fangs during mating

WC – wild caught

Chapter One: Understanding Tarantulas

Tarantulas are not like most mainstream pets – nor should they be treated as one. They are predatory, venomous, dangerous, territorial, and while many of the tarantulas being kept are being touted as docile and non-aggressive, under the right circumstances, even the most docile of these creatures can turn aggressive or defensive. And they are certainly well-equipped to defend themselves.

This book covers much of the practical aspects you will need to know in caring for a tarantula. It is recommended that you do not stop at this book, but to use this as a starting point for further research. One should never undertake the responsibility of keeping a tarantula as a pet without knowing what it is they are getting into.

Facts About Tarantulas

There are over 800 species of tarantulas scattered all over the world, and many are far too dangerous to be kept as pets. There are, however, some beginner species that are recommended for novice tarantula keepers – chosen because of their docile and non-aggressive temperament, as well as the relative ease of their care.

Some have called tarantulas low maintenance pets, but this can be a little misleading. You need to provide them with an appropriate habitat that needs to be regularly maintained in terms of cleanliness, temperatures and humidity levels. They also need to be fed live prey – insects for the most part. Given these essentials of tarantula keeping, yes, tarantulas are low maintenance pets. They take up little space, are quiet, and require hardly any socialization or training at all.

They are beautiful to look at, certainly, and fascinating to watch. But one must never forget, even after months or years of keeping them securely locked inside their cages, that these are dangerous creatures and thus deserves the corresponding respect and caution.

Summary of Tarantula Facts

Basic Tarantula Information

Kingdom: Animalia

Phylum: Arthropoda

Subphylum: Chelicerata

Class: Arachnida

Order: Araneae

Infraorder: Mygalomorphae

Family: Theraphosidae

Regions of Origin: United States, Central, South America, Africa, Asia, Australia, Spain, Portugal, Turkey, Italy, Cyprus

Primary Habitat: Varies depending on the species and region of origin, but can include savannahs, grasslands, rainforests, deserts, scrublands, mountains, and forest, in tropical and subtropical climates; they can either be terrestrial and burrowers in the ground, or arboreal and tree-dwelling

Description: Most are black or brown, but some species have more vivid coloring such as blue, orange, or yellow. They have 8 closely grouped eyes (2 large eyes surrounded by 3 eyes on each side; their bodies have two major parts – the prosoma and the abdomen, that is connected by a pedicle which allows the two parts to move independently. Tarantulas, unlike true spiders, have fangs that point straight down instead of sideways. They have 8 legs, and their legs and abdomen are covered by thick hair.

Primary Behavioral Characteristics: Nocturnal, territorial, predatory, cannibalistic; can either be burrowers or arboreal

Health Conditions: Dehydration, Losing a leg, Bleeding and injuries, Bad molting, Internal infection from mold and fungus, Parasites

Lifespan: on the average, tarantulas can live up to 30 years

Origin and Distribution

There are over 850 different species of Tarantulas or spiders belonging to the Theraphosidae family spread all over the world, from countries and continents as diverse as the United States, Central America, South America, Africa, Asia, Australia, and Europe.

The name itself derives from the Italian "tarantola," from "Taranto" – a seaport city of Southern Italy where spiders were quite common. The name was originally used to refer to a species of wolf spider native to Mediterranean Europe, but subsequently, the name was used as a generic term for any large, ground-dwelling spider. Eventually, "tarantula" was used to refer to any large or hairy spider, and no longer used to refer to the wolf spiders.

Today, the term "tarantula" is used to refer to any spider belonging to the family Theraphosidae, which are often large and hairy arachnids. They have since been quite popular in the exotic pet trade.

Chapter Two: Things to Know Before Getting a Tarantula

They may not be everybody's first choice, but for others, tarantulas make ideal pets. They are small, quiet, exotic, fascinating, and beautiful in a deadly and venomous kind of way. But for these very same reasons, one should consider carefully before actually bringing one home.

Having any kind of pet means responsibility for the life of another living thing, and more so for an exotic species which necessarily requires extra effort in learning about them, caring for them, while at the same time giving them the respect that they are due.

Caring for a venomous and potentially dangerous species also means being socially responsible to the people around us who might come into contact with these creatures. More importantly, having a tarantula for a pet means learning what it means to care for one, and then putting in the time, effort, and even monetary investment to really care for one long term. Having any pet means caring for them for the duration of their lives – not just immediately after satisfying your whim for having such an exotic pet.

In this chapter, we take a look at some of the more practical aspects of caring for a pet tarantula, and include some basic considerations such as licensing, costs, and the pros and cons of keeping a pet tarantula – factors that really should be looked into before making any final decision about bringing a pet tarantula home.

Do You Need a License?

There are no national or federal laws prohibiting keeping tarantulas as pets, and many state laws are quiet about pet tarantulas as opposed to other, more common pets. Still, the only way to really be sure is to do your research. Licensing laws and permits regarding pets are usually decided on the state or local level, and these can change over time, and quite quickly, at that.

Do your research with your local legislature regarding any licensing requirements for the keeping of tarantulas as pets – as well as their transport and import/export – especially if you plan on traveling with them, or are purchasing them from outside the state or country. Legitimate breeders/exporters usually require a US Fish and Wildlife import/export license (USFW) before they can ship tarantulas into the United States.

Even if state laws are quiet regarding pet tarantulas, it is advisable that you expand your research into local municipal, city, town, and even neighborhood rules because these might provide further regulations regarding pet tarantulas even when state law otherwise allows it. Make sure that you are not violating any of your state or local laws.

How Many Tarantulas Should You Keep?

As a general rule, Tarantulas should be kept in separate containers, so whether or not you can keep more than one Tarantula should depend on your capacity to provide them with well-equipped enclosures and, of course, your ability to care for them and maintain their environments.

While there are more advanced hobbyists and keepers who can responsibly provide a communal set up for their tarantulas – this is not really recommended for beginners. You would have to have several years of experience with each particular specie to make sure that keeping more than one of them together will not result in aggression, fights, or cases of cannibalism. Regardless of what information you may gather about each species and how they treat each other, one can never be sure when it comes to individual spiders – particularly ones kept in captivity and in close proximity to each other. If you really are aiming to keep more than one Tarantula, make sure you have species-specific enclosures for each of them. Don't attempt a communal setup unless you have done extensive research and have several years of experience in keeping and caring for tarantulas.

Do Tarantulas Get Along with Other Pets?

Needless to say, a potentially venomous and dangerous creature such as a tarantula should never be allowed too much contact with other pets – especially mammals that can prove too eager and that might pose a threat to the tarantula, who might then react aggressively or defensively. While the venom of many beginner tarantulas are not always fatal to humans, the same cannot be said for the effects of their venom on smaller mammals.

Other pets such as smaller mammals, and even reptiles, should in no case be allowed contact with your tarantula. Some adult tarantulas can feed off of small reptiles in the wild, as well as the young of small mammals such as mice. The potential danger is also true in reverse; that is, larger pets such as dogs, cats, or even mice and reptiles, can also cause harm to your pet tarantula, causing them injury or even eating them outright.

Bottom line, tarantulas should never be allowed outside of their enclosure unsupervised, and should in no case be allowed to mingle with other pets.

How Much Does it Cost to Keep a Tarantula?

The cost of a purchase of a tarantula primarily depends on which species you are getting. As a general average, however, a good starter or beginner tarantula can cost anywhere from $10 to upwards of $500 for an adult of a more rare species. Startup costs could average around $95, broken down as follows:

Startup costs for a Pet Tarantula	
Purchase price	$20
10 gallon aquarium	$20
Light fixture	$20
Bulb	$10
Automatic timer	$10
Cage accessories (substrate, starter burrows, water dish, etc.)	$15
Total	$95

Of course, this is quite apart from the yearly maintenance, around which you can probably expect to spend around $90 each year. These would involve costs for the following:

Yearly Maintenance Costs	
Food	$50
Lamp bulbs	$20
Cage accessories	$20
Total	$90

Of course, these are just general estimates, and you may find yourself spending more or less depending on your unique circumstances and the available resources in your area. One other potential costs you should consider investing in are good reference books covering the actual species you are looking to purchase, as well as good reference books regarding tarantulas and tarantula care in particular. These latter are likely to be your more expensive purchases, but for the truly dedicated hobbyist or keeper, they can also be your most important investment.

What are the Pros and Cons of Keeping Tarantulas as Pets

There are pros and cons to keeping tarantulas as pets, and this can tip the scales for some in either direction. Fact is, tarantulas make great pets for some, but not for others. Whether they will make great pets for you or not depends on whether you want to keep a pet tarantula in the first place, and whether or not your lifestyle allows you to effectively keep and care for one of these fascinating creatures.

Below we have provided a bullet-list of the various pros and cons to keeping a pet tarantula which can enable you to effectively assess your capacity of being a tarantula keeper, and whether or not a tarantula is really the best kind of pet for you.

Pros for the Tarantula

- Small pets that take up little space – a good choice for apartment pets
- Quiet and odorless – great for people with allergies
- Low maintenance pets – you don't need to walk them or litter-train them
- They don't need daily feeding
- Can be fascinating, inspirational, and educational creatures for children interested in the natural sciences
- Beautiful, interesting, and fascinating animals – great conversation starters, have amazing and vivid colors
- Inexpensive to maintain
- A long life span – some can live up to 20 or more years
- Requires little to no socialization

Cons for the Tarantula

- You will need to deal with bugs and other insects, and occasionally feed them live prey
- You should care for them diligently – no putting off of regular care and maintenance

- Could be intimidating or frightening for other people – especially those with arachnophobia
- They aren't cuddly animals – won't be affectionate and won't like being handled too much or too often
- Are venomous – can be dangerous if not handled correctly, and their venom can be lethal for those with allergies
- Many tarantulas have more than one mode of protection – they can flick or urticate hairs when threatened
- Will not get along well with other household pets
- Certain states may prohibit the purchase or possession of spiders, particularly venomous spiders

Chapter Three: Ten Best Tarantula Pets for Beginners

The choice to keep a Tarantula Spider as a pet is not one to be taken lightly, and with that comes the choice of which species is right for you.

The choice is nearly infinite with more than 800 species the world over. In general, they require little space, and are pretty easy to care for – but it would still depend on the species. And of course, tarantulas have a dangerous reputation, many species of which actually live up to.

This is why it is important to do your research beforehand, and this is doubly more important if you are a beginner at keeping pet tarantulas. While most have venomous bites, their venom is not usually enough to kill a person. But this isn't true for all species. Some people can have a strong allergic reaction to the tarantula venom, and some species have venom that can be fatal for humans. Being wild animals, the first thing you should do if you are planning on keeping one as a pet is to treat them with the respect they are due.

With so many tarantula species to choose from, how do you know which is the best one for you? In this chapter, we cover ten beginner tarantulas that have become popular for first time owners. Most of these are ground dwellers, and are preferred because they tend to be slower moving compared to arboreal types.

1. *Chilean Rose (Grammostola rosea)*

The Chilean Rose Tarantula or the Grammostola rosea, also sometimes known as the rose hair tarantula, the Chilean Fire Tarantula, or the Chilean Red-haired tarantula, is one of the most common beginner tarantula pets available.

For one thing, they are hardy and docile, easy to care for, and are inexpensive and are one of the more commonly tarantula species available in American and European pet stores. This is on account of the large numbers of wild caught Chilean rose tarantulas exported from their native Chile into the pet trade.

Origin: Chile, Bolivia and Argentina

Size: 4-5 – 5-5 inches

Natural Habitat: burrows in desert and scrub regions

Recommended Habitat: small 5-10 gallon tank, with a width 2-3 times wider than the spider's leg span, and a height equivalent to the spider's leg span. Provide 2-3 inches or substrate made from moss, soil or vermiculite, a shelter or retreat for hiding made of wood or a small clay flower pot.

Habitat Requirements: Keep at temperatures of 70-85 F (21-30 C) and humidity levels of 60-70%

Diet: Insects such as grasshoppers, moths, beetles, cockroaches, mealworms, and for full grown spiders, occasional pinkies. In the wild, they also feed on small lizards and mammals.

Handling: Docile and skittish, but can become aggressive if handled too frequently

Lifespan: 15-20 years, or longer

2. *Mexican Redleg (Brachypelma smithi)*

Also known as the red-legged tarantula, the Mexican Redleg is distinctive for having a dark-colored body with the second joint of its leg as either pink, red, or orange. Its carapace is lightly-colored, and it has a black triangle at the front.

This is another popular species among tarantula keepers because of its docile temperament, its unique coloration, and its impressive size.

Origin: Mexico and Panama

Size: 5-6 inches legspan

Natural Habitat: scrublands

Recommended Habitat: 5-10 gallon tank with a locking screen top, with an under-tank heat pad. Provide a substrate about two inches deep, a hide area, and a shallow water dish

Habitat Requirements: Keep at temperatures of 75-85 F(24-30 C) and humidity levels at 65-70%

Diet: Gut-loaded crickets, mealworms, or waxworms, with an occasional pinkie for larger spiders

Handling: Relative docile and skittish, and very reluctant to bite even with distressed. It protects itself mainly by flicking urticating hair when threatened

Lifespan: males can live up to 5 years, females may live until 20 – 30 years

3. *Mexican Redknee (Brachypelma smithi)*

Distinctive for their vibrant colors and "red knees," the Mexican Redknee is another popular choice among tarantula hobbyists. These are a large species with a long lifespan, and are now considered to be the "classic" pet tarantula.

Generally docile, they are only slightly venomous to humans, and can kick urticating hairs from their abdomens if threatened.

This species has been bred successfully in captivity over the years. Unfortunately, their numbers in the wild have declined due to excessive exports of wild caught specimens to the Chinese market, as well as systematic extermination by the local populace. The Mexican Redknee was listed as endangered by CITES in 1985.

Origin: western faces of the Sierra Madre Occidental and Sierra Madre del Sur mountain ranges in Mexico, particularly the tropical rain forests in Colima and Guerrero

Size: 5-5.5 inches legspan

Natural Habitat: deep burrows in soil banks near vegetation in deciduous tropical forests

Recommended Habitat: 5-10 gallon tank with a width 2-3 times wider than the legspan, and height twice as tall as the leg span, equipped with substrate that is at least half the height of the terrarium to give them enough space for burrowing

Habitat Requirements: Keep at temperatures of 75-80 F (24-30 C) and humidity levels at 50-60%

Diet: Crickets and other large insects, smaller insects, and adults will occasionally eat pinkies, lizards, and even a mouse

Handling: Generally docile and calm, hardy and colorful

Lifespan: females can live from 15-25 years, or even up to 30 years

4. *Honduran Curly Hair Tarantula (Brachypelma albopilosum)*

Also sometimes known as the Curly Hair Tarantulas or Wooly Tarantulas, this species are another popular beginner tarantulas among hobbyists for their docile and calm temperament.

This spider is so called because of their characteristic long hair with a characteristic curl. They are generally plump, with dark brown to black hair, and a golden-bronze sheen because of longer gold hairs all over its body.

This is a nocturnal species that hunts by ambushing its prey, using its venom to paralyze its victim as well as beginning digestion. Afterwards, the Curly hair tarantula sucks up its prey's proteins and fats until only remnants of undigested parts are left.

Even though this species has been bred successfully in captivity, please take note that this species is listed in the CITES convention due to their diminishing numbers in the wild. Currently, international trade is only allowed via trade permits and according to quotas.

Origin: Costa Rica

Size: 5-5.5 inches legspan

Natural Habitat: burrows in tropical scrublands, living around the base of large trees, near rivers, or in patches of cleared rain forest

Recommended Habitat: 5-10 gallon tank with a width 2-3 times wider than the legspan, and height twice as tall as the leg span, equipped with substrate that should be at least 3-4 inches

Habitat Requirements: Keep at temperatures of 70-85 F (25-30 C) and humidity levels at 65-80%

Diet: Crickets and other large insects, smaller insects, and adults will occasionally eat pinkies, lizards, and even a mouse

Handling: Generally docile, gentle, and calm, hardy and colorful, but will kick urticating hairs from its abdomen when threatened

Lifespan: females can live from 3-10 years, with males generally living for a shorter lifespan

5. *Pink Zebra Beauty (Eualaestrus campestratus)*

A brownish-black tarantula with yellow striped markings near the knees, the Pink Zebra beauty is a popular pet tarantula among beginners because of its docile and tolerant temperament. It's a hardy species of tarantula, and slow moving, and is ideal for beginning hobbyists because it is not quick on the offensive – whether to bite, or to urticate hair.

More commonly known as the Pink Zebra Beauty, it is often confused with the Chaco Golden Knee. But its distinguishing characteristic is the brownish-black and yellow striped markings near the knees, as opposed to the whitish markings on the Chaco Golden Knee.

Origin: Brazil, Paraguay and Argentina

Size: 5-6 inches legspan

Natural Habitat: grasslands and savannahs

Recommended Habitat: 5-10 gallon tank with a width 2-3 times wider than the legspan, and height twice as tall as the leg span, equipped with substrate that should be at least 4 inches, equipped with a piece of bark to serve as a starter burrow hide

Habitat Requirements: Keep at temperatures of 75-80 F (24-30 C) and humidity levels at 70%

Diet: Crickets and smaller insects, occasionally adults will eat a pinkie

Handling: Very docile, and hardly ever hisses or attempts to bite

Lifespan: males can live from 8-10 years, while females can live from 18-25 years

6. *Costa Rican Zebra (Aphonoplema seemanni)*

Sometimes called the Striped-Knee Tarantula, this tarantula is black with distinctive white stripes near its joints ("knees"), which accounts for its name. Occasionally, brown coloration with tan striping may also occur – usually occurring among those that come from Nicaragua. In the wild, they are often found in large aggregations.

This is a beautiful tarantula species that is popular among hobbyists because it is quite hardy, and comparatively inexpensive compared to other species. It is also quite docile, but also quite fast. They can be quite adept at escaping.

Origin: Costa Rica and other parts of Central America, including Honduras, Nicaragua, and Guatemala

Size: 4-4.5 inches legspan

Natural Habitat: deep burrows in open and semi-arid scrublands and tropical rainforests

Recommended Habitat: 5-10 gallon tank with a width 2-3 times wider than the legspan, and height twice as tall as the leg span, equipped with substrate that should be at least 4 inches, equipped with a piece of bark to serve as a starter burrow hide

Habitat Requirements: Keep at temperatures of 70-85 F (25-30 C) and humidity levels at 75-80%

Diet: Insects such as grasshoppers, cockroaches, and crickets, with adults occasionally eating pinkies

Handling: Quite docile and a bit skittish, which probably accounts for their incredible speed! Too much handling is therefore not recommended

Lifespan: males usually live up to 5 years, females can live up to 20 years

7. *Pinktoe Tarantula (Avicularia versicolor)*

Native to Costa Rica, Brazil and the southern Carribean, this beautiful tarantula species is also sometimes called Guyana pinktoe, Common pinktoe, or South American pinktoe. As its name implies, this species is distinctive for its pinkish feet, which presents a contrast to its dark black or metallic gray with deep violet/reddish-colored body. This is a more interesting species to keep because aside from its unique coloring, they are also known to build extensive web tubes within their enclosures.

This is an arboreal or tree-dwelling species, and so require more vertical room in their habitat, with plenty of climbing space. The good news is that they are quite docile, though they can be active and fast moving. Their venom is considered mild compared to other species.

The pinktoe usually runs or retreats when threatened, though it will defend itself when provoked. One interesting fact about this tarantula is that their preferred method of hunting is by stationization, which is remaining completely still until the actual moment of attack.

Origin: Costa Rica, Brazil, Trinidad, French Guyana, Surinam, Venezuela, the Amazon Basin, and the southern Carribean

Size: 4.5 – 5 inches

Natural Habitat: this is an arboreal or tree-dwelling species

Recommended Habitat: A large, vertically oriented enclosure, 2-3 inches of substrate and live plants to help maintain humidity as well as provide places to climb. A shallow water dish can help maintain humidity levels, while sufficient ventilation keeps bacteria from developing in the moist or humid environment

Habitat Requirements: Keep at temperatures of 78-82 F and humidity levels at 65-75%

Diet: Crickets, moths, flies, other large insects, and adults will occasionally eat a small lizard or a pinkie

Handling: Handle gently and carefully! They are quite docile, but fast, and will become agitated and quite likely to jump if nervous or when handled roughly. Beware that this species also tends to spray a small amount of fecal matter as a defense mechanism

Lifespan: males can live from 2-3 years, while females can live as long as 8-12 years

8. Green Bottle Blue Tarantula (Chromatopelma cyaneopubescens)

This species has some of the most dramatic coloring you will see among the various tarantula species – metallic blue legs, a blue green carapace, and abdomen of vibrant orange color. For this reason, among others, they are one of the most popular tarantula species among hobbyists.

Aptly named the Greenbottle Blue Tarantula (though sometimes also called the Orange & Blue Bottlebrush or the Venezuelan Bottlebrush, these tarantulas live in webbed burrows resembling tunnels underneath tree roots and bushes in desert areas – be prepared to find their enclosure filled with these tunnel-like webbings. They can be quite territorial about their burrows, and while calm and docile, they can also be skittish. They will either run quickly when disturbed, or will go on the offensive if their burrows are threatened.

Unlike most slow moving and shy tarantulas, this species can be interesting to observe and watch. They are resilient and easy to care for, so they make great beginner pets. They grow quickly and are voracious feeders, though constant handling is not recommended because while hardy, their skittishness can often cause them injury. A fall could potentially rupture their abdomen and kill them.

Origin: Paraguana peninsula and Venezuela

Size: 4.5 – 6 inches

Natural Habitat: tree and land dwellings (semi arboreal) in harsh and dry climate in desert areas

Recommended Habitat: 5-10 gallon tank with a width 2-3 times wider than the legspan, and height twice as tall as the leg span. Recommended substrate is 4-6 inches of shredded coconut fiber or coir, though top soil or peat will work just as well.

Habitat Requirements: Keep at temperatures of 80-90 F and humidity levels at 40-60%

Diet: Crickets, moths, flies, other small insects, mealworms and wax worms, though adults will often eat insects as large as themselves

Handling: This is another docile and skittish species, and would much rather run when disturbed

Lifespan: males can live from 2-4 years, while females can live from 12-13 years

9. *Brazilian Black Tarantula (Grammostola pulchra)*

This is a terrestrial tarantula commonly known as the Brazilian black due to its almost entirely rich, black velvety hair and coloring. They are quite gentle and docile in temperament, and would much rather flee than attack. You might notice them burrowing immediately after being disturbed. Though please remember that like most tarantulas, they will defend themselves if provoked – using their venom or urticating hairs. The Black's venom, however, is not as irritating as that of many other tarantula species.

They can be quite expensive because of their desirability as pets (they are much less prone to kick urticating hairs when handled), the long lives of the mature females, and a ban on the export of wild caught specimens.

Origin: Brazil and north of Uruguay

Size: up to 8 inches legspan

Natural Habitat: This is a terrestrial and opportunistic burrower type that lives in the Brazil and Uruguay grasslands

Recommended Habitat: 10-15 gallon enclosure with a good ventilation and secure lid, equip with 4-5 inches of substrate made of coir or dry potting soil, with a bark to serve as a starter burrow. This species also seems to enjoy basking near light.

Habitat Requirements: Keep at temperatures of 75-85 F and humidity levels at 60-70%

Diet: Opportunistic eaters, Brazilian Blacks eat crickets, roach nymphs, and other small insects

Handling: Generally calm and docile but active, making them great beginner tarantula pets; they are quite hardy and tolerant of handling. They usually don't bite, and their venom is relatively mild, but the fangs of an adult are large enough that they can do enough physical damage without the venom.

Lifespan: males can live from 5-6 years, while females can live up to 20 or more years

10. Chaco Golden Knee (Grammostola pulchripes)

Somewhat akin to a gentle giant, this large tarantula species is also known for its calm and docile temperament, making it a very popular pet tarantula among beginner hobbyists. This is also a great pet to look at – they aren't shy about being out on display, and the species sports flashy light-colored hairs all over its body, with gold stripes on its legs and knees.

Caring for a Chaco Golden Knee is pretty straightforward, and they can live up to 15 years or longer. Their colors seem to become more vivid as they mature, and they tend to be a laid back species that is not at all shy but is rather quite friendly and open.

Origin: The Chaco region of Argentina and in the Grand Chaco in Paraguay

Size: up to 8 inches or more in legspan

Natural Habitat: This is a terrestrial and opportunistic burrower type that lives in the grasslands of Argentina and Paraguay

Recommended Habitat: At least 15 gallon terrarium equipped with a shelter or starter burrow made from a large piece of bark or plastic hut, with a thick layer of substrate, at least 6 inches.

Habitat Requirements: Keep at temperatures of 78 F and humidity levels at 65%

Diet: Crickets, roaches, grasshoppers and other small insects

Handling: One of the most calm, docile, and hardy species in the trade, be aware that like many other tarantulas, they can still defend themselves – usually by flicking urticating hairs when alarmed. Try not to startle them by sudden movements or too much handling, especially early on.

Lifespan: males can live from 5-6 years, while females can live up to 15 or more years

Chapter Four: Purchasing Your Tarantula

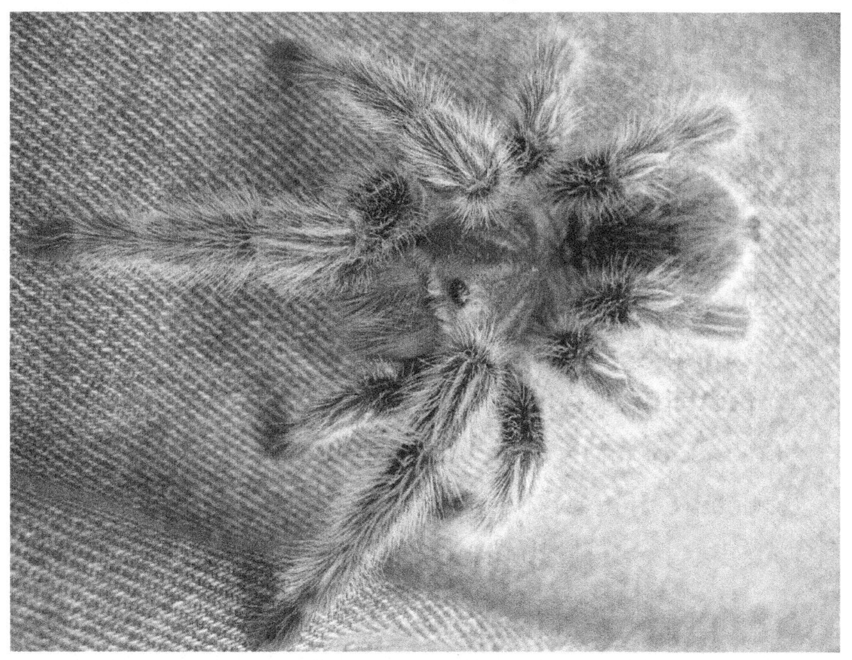

Tarantulas aren't what you might call "mainstream" pets, and so finding them might not be easy. In some states, commercial establishments may even be prohibited from selling venomous animals without the necessary license or permits. In recent years, enterprising individuals intent on having a pet tarantula have therefore had to expand their search – to private vendors from as far afield as out of state and sometimes outside of the country.

These days, thankfully, there have been an increasing number of tarantula breeders which means that the supply of pet tarantulas available in the market has also increased.

This is good news because purchasing wild caught tarantulas is no longer advisable. Some countries have prohibited the export of their native species of tarantula that have been classified as threatened or endangered – likely a result of too many specimens being caught for the pet trade. And in any case, sticking to captive bred tarantulas is more advisable – especially for novice tarantula keepers. Captive bred tarantulas are less likely to be carrying parasites, and are more acclimated (therefore more tolerant) to conditions of captivity and the presence of humans. When you are looking for a place to purchase your tarantula, therefore, try to ensure that you are not supporting illegal pet trades by purchasing wild caught tarantulas.

With the advent of the Internet and the growing popularity of non-mainstream pets such as the tarantula, the prospective owner now has several options in looking for a place to buy their own tarantula.

How to Choose a Reputable Tarantula Breeder

While the first (and only) local option that many people have is to visit their local pet stores, this may not always be a feasible source. Many pet stores operate and are driven by profit, and many a conscientious hobbyist finds himself or herself appalled at the conditions at which the animals are kept. And this is particularly true of creatures such as tarantulas that require specific care, and which store employees that handle a bunch of animals each day may not be able to provide. Some may feel compelled to "rescue" these animals by purchasing them and providing them with the home and the care they need, but this is not a viable long-term proposition. The more animals you buy from such pet stores can only promote their business, and thus encourage them to stock up on more of these creatures. And not even the most conscientious individual can "rescue" every single tarantula they come across. The same is true for most other animals that pet stores sell – responsible pet owners generally avoid supporting businesses, and indirectly, the breeders that sell to them – that are driven more by profit than genuine care for the animals. The so-called "puppy mills" may not be isolated to dog breeders alone.

Thankfully, the Internet has seen the growth in popularity and networking opportunities among tarantula hobbyists and breeders. Be sure to read the reviews and testimonials of people who have already bought tarantulas from specific breeders to get an idea of the type of breeders you might be dealing with. Then after you make contact, don't hesitate to ask questions – breeders that are genuinely passionate about the animals they sell will not be averse to answering any questions you may have. Many will even be open to an on-site visit to their set-up, and be willing to entertain genuine enthusiasts. The good news is that many of these breeders that advertise and sell online also ship the tarantulas directly to your doorstep. This is viable if you cannot travel long distances to visit their facilities. If so, the only option you have of vetting the breeder is through phone or online messages and reviews. Just be objective, be respectful, and don't forget to do your own research.

Another option you may have is to visit tarantula exhibitions where hobbyists, keepers and breeders come to buy, sell, and generally network with each other regarding their common interest in tarantulas. This can be a great place to find like-minded people, share your interests in a pet that may not be universally loved by everyone, and to establish great networking opportunities with breeders from whom you may buy, ask questions, and possibly even sell or trade some of your own tarantulas.

Tips for Selecting a Healthy Tarantula

It is assumed that you have already selected the tarantula species you prefer – based on your capacity to care for them and your experience level. If not, please see Chapter Three on the ten best tarantula pets for beginners.

We reiterate here our suggestion that you buy only captive bred – not wild caught – tarantulas. As to gender, many keepers prefer buying females because they generally have longer lifespans than the males. Of course, if you are looking to breed your own tarantulas, you may be actively looking for a male of a particular species. But if you are not looking to breed tarantulas, and wish only to purchase a single tarantula for a pet, then females generally provide longer-term satisfaction simply because they live longer. Just be aware that while sexed males may be cheaper, they will probably die in the next six months to two years, while the more expensive female tarantulas can often live up to 15-20 years or longer. It really depends on what you are looking for.

The next thing you have to consider is whether you are buying an adult, a juvenile, or a sling. Slings or spiderlings are cheaper, but they are also more fragile, more difficult to feed, and more likely to die while molting. However, they can be a wonderful opportunity to actually see the growth and development of a tarantula from youth to adult, and the watching the incredible changes they go through can be a fascinating, exciting, and gratifying journey.

If you purchase adult tarantulas, on the other hand, you are getting a tarantula that is at least a bit more hardy than spiderlings. They do not require such delicate care as the slings, will not have to be fed regularly, and are generally easier to care for. Of course, they will be more expensive than the spiderlings.

Now that you know which species to get, and at which life stage, you should ask yourself how to pick a healthy tarantula. Below are some tips and guidelines to keep in mind as you make your choice:

- While some tarantulas are naturally shy, they are always alert. They'll be ready to run if you make any sudden moves, and they will certainly be wary at the approach of a human. But if you find them just lurking in a corner, unmoving, completely exposed, with its legs tucked up underneath it, then chances are good that it is sick and might even be dying.
- In the same vein, try to avoid tarantulas that are hunched over with their legs curled under them, or that seem incredibly thin. This could be an indication of dehydration. Also avoid tarantulas that have unhealthy-looking cream-colored splotches scattered over their body – this could be an indication of an infection from unclean water.
- Bare or bald patches on a tarantula's abdomen indicates where it has kicked up urticating hairs. If you are wary of buying a tarantula that kicks up its hairs too often, this could be a warning sign for you, and you might want to look for a seemingly more

docile species. But the truth is that after molting, all that hair will come back in all its glory, and is not a sure indication of a docile tarantula. On the other hand, if you are concerned because of the bald patch (say you want a full abdomen of hair on that abdomen), don't worry about it. It will grow back after the next molt. The same is true of any missing legs – provided the leg has healed cleanly, of course.

Chapter Five: Caring for Your New Tarantula

Tarantulas may be considered as low maintenance pets – but this assumes that you have provided them the appropriate set up in terms of housing or cage requirements. And even then, regular maintenance is still a must in terms of cleaning up within the cage and regularly monitoring the temperature and humidity levels within their artificial habitat. It is therefore important to ensure that you have the proper set up before you even consider bringing your tarantula home. If done right in the very beginning, you might not have to do much other than regular cleaning and maintenance.

Please remember that it is never advisable to keep more than one tarantula in the same cage or habitat. Even among species that may be considered communal, tarantulas can often be territorial and cannibalistic, and they can show aggression towards each other, resulting in fights, violence, and sometimes even outright attacks where the loser is fed upon by the victor.

Setting up the Tarantula Habitat

Tarantulas are notorious escape artists, and many can move more quickly than even your eyes can follow. Ensure against possible escape by getting a terrarium or tank with a secure lid that is properly ventilated, or you can choose one with a locking mesh screen top. This will do well to make ensure that your tarantula is secure will not be able to escape. Of course, if you are keeping spiderlings or slings, you need to make sure that those little guys will not fit through the ventilation holes to escape. As a general rule, don't choose a cage where the ventilation holes are not bigger than the tarantula's carapace.

The size of the enclosure should neither be too big nor too large. The height and width should be no bigger than 2-3 times the legspan of the tarantula. The actual height of the interior is variable depending on the species. Terrestrial tarantulas need no more than a legspan in the height of their enclosure, while arboreal species need more vertical space – though this can be easily adjusted with the depth of the substrate that you use. Clear, plastic containers are ideal – they are inexpensive, and they allow you to see clearly inside and observe your tarantula and the interior of the cage to check that everything is clean and in good order.

Equip the tank or terrarium with sufficient substrate – 3-4 inches is a good depth for many burrowing tarantulas, though you should certainly make adjustments depending on the species you have. The larger the tarantula, the deeper the substrate that is needed. On the other hand, if you are keeping an arboreal or tree dwelling species, you can afford a more shallow substrate depth (around 1-3 inches) and increase the vertical space inside the habitat to make way for climbing space. Provide them with places to climb inside the cage such as a plastic plant or a tree bark. Just be careful of "tall" structures within the cage that reach near the lid – arboreal tarantulas may weave silken webs or nests aboveground, so be careful when opening the cage that the tarantula does not escape.

There are many options for substrate – and many hobbyists like to mix up different materials such as sterilized potting soil, crushed coconut fiber (coconut coir), horticultural vermiculite, or peat moss, etc. Just make sure that it is pesticide and fertilizer free. Keep the substrate moist, but do not saturate it with water – you can do this by keeping the bottom depth of the substrate damp, while the upper portion dry except for perhaps a slightly damp corner.

Finally, as you put the finishing touches on your tarantula's home, keep in mind the functionality of everything you put in: live plants are both aesthetically pleasing and can also help in maintaining humidity levels, various plants, rocks, logs, or tree barks can also serve as a starter burrow or a hide area for your pet.

Finally, it is not necessary to provide specific lighting requirements for your tarantula's habitat. They don't really need it, and many tarantulas do not like bright lights. In fact, lighting can actually dry out the cage's interior. If you do want light, select a low-wattage fixture with a red light.

Locate the enclosure in place that is safe and secure – where they will not be under direct sunlight and is free from drafts. Make sure that they will not be disturbed by other pets such as dogs and cats, and that they will not be in the way of too much comings and goings, or be subject to loud disturbances.

Temperature and Humidity Requirements

Temperature and humidity requirements are generally species-specific. Depending on which species of tarantula you have, and which type of habitat they come from, they may require different levels of temperature. You would not provide the same type of habitat to a species that is native to a desert region as you would to a species whose native habitat is all forests and grasslands. So together with conducting careful research into which species of tarantula would serve you best in terms of your lifestyle, the type of care they would need, and their temperament, comes also the research into their native habitat. The enclosure or habitat you provide them should approximate their native habitat as closely as possible.

As a general rule, however, temperatures for tarantulas should be kept somewhere between 70-80 F, with nighttime temperatures a bit cooler but in no case exceeding 80 degrees for extended periods of time. A fluctuating room temperature in a warm home is best. Just keep in mind that the warmer you keep your tarantula, the faster the metabolism is. They will have greater appetite, and they will grow faster, but it also means that the substrate will dry faster and they might be more prone to dehydration. Use your best judgment, and pay close attention to what seems best for your individual tarantula.

Keeping Your Tarantula Happy and Healthy

A tarantula is a pretty hardy creature, and much of the possible illnesses that they could suffer in captivity is generally the result of poor husbandry – a poor or insufficient diet, for instance, but most importantly, poor living conditions.

It is important to keep your tarantula's cage clean and well-maintained. Cage maintenance should be done every day: clean their water dish and replace the water with fresh clear water each day, and remove any exoskeleton, uneaten food or remnants of food. Pay attention to the humidity levels – many tarantulas die from too much moisture than they do from dehydration – molds or fungus could begin to grow in your pet's cage if it is too moist, and this could signal the beginnings of contamination and then infection. If the cage is too dry, daily misting with a substrate that holds moisture is a quick solution. And if you feed your tarantula live prey – they should be removed if uneaten because there is also a chance that they could attack your tarantula instead – a definite possibility particularly when your tarantula is molting and thus extremely vulnerable.

Every 4-6 months (or more often if necessary), give the enclosure a deep and thorough cleaning. Move your tarantula to a temporary holding container before doing so. Then remove all the contents of the tank, wash and sterilize the inside and outside of the tank, replace the substrate, clean the water dish, and clean and sterilize all the items inside the tank before replacing them.

Chapter Six: Feeding Your Tarantula

Feeding your tarantula is perhaps one of the more straightforward aspects of their care. As your spider grows, the frequency of its feeding will grow less, and some adults can thrive on feeding once or twice a week – some can even go through a period of fasting and live for months without feeding. As long as you aren't squeamish about handling live prey – which is mostly what a tarantula's diet consists of.

Neither do you have to worry about overfeeding your pet tarantula. There has simply been no scientific proof of this. They are perfectly capable of regulating their own feeding, and will simply not touch the food you give them if they don't need it. When this happens, simply remove the prey from the cage. Some tarantulas can go for months without feeding, and this is no cause for immediate alarm.

The Basics of a Tarantula's Diet

What a tarantula eats is varied: you have the option of feeding them grasshoppers, crickets, moths, beetle larvae, houseflies, cockroaches, and earthworms. Larger tarantulas also eat pinkies (or live baby rodents), lizards, and even sometimes snakes. Needless to say, your tarantula should have ready access to fresh and clean water at all times.

Whatever you choose to feed your tarantula, make sure that the food has not been exposed to any chemicals or pesticides. This is why most recommend against feeding wild caught insects unless there is absolute certainty that the prey has not been exposed to any pesticides. Fortunately, a good selection of cultivated prey items are now commercially available. Crickets are often considered the food of choice for many keepers and hobbyists simply because they are easier to come by. Many pet stores sell these insects, and they can even be purchased in bulk. This is the same for mealworms, and some feeder roaches are also available to purchase online.

Many tarantulas in captivity do fine on a steady diet of crickets, supplemented every so often with other insects. Occasionally, the larger specimens can be given small lizards or pinkie mice if so desired. The most important thing to keep in mind is that you should never feed your tarantula prey that is larger than itself. On the average, anything that is smaller than the length and width of its abdomen is suitable. The reason for this is that tarantulas can sometimes be aggressive feeders, and they will wrestle with their food even though they no longer to feed. Many will feed pre-killed prey that has been suitably chopped up into appropriate sizes in order to meet this requirement.

Gut Loading Crickets

In order to ensure that your tarantula gets its fill of a nutritious diet, many keepers "gut load" the crickets before feeding them to their pets. This consists of putting the cricket on a diet of nutritious food that is also dusted with vitamins just before being fed to your tarantula. Doing so ensures that your tarantula also benefits from the food and nutrition that you provide the cricket. There are many options for cricket food that are commercially available.

Tips for Feeding Your Tarantula

Because of how seldom a tarantula (especially an adult) eats, the danger in feeding them live prey is that sometimes the prey can turn on the tarantula itself. This is particularly true before, during, and immediately after molting when your tarantula will not be eating and is also extremely vulnerable. Check the cage each day and if the food remains uneaten, remove them. Even if the prey doesn't turn on the tarantula, leaving food items in the cage can be dangerous because it becomes the breeding ground of bacteria, pests and mold that can eventually harm your tarantula or make them sick.

The frequency of feeding depends on your tarantula's current stage of growth, and on how fast you want them to grow. Younger spiders (slings and spiderlings) must be fed at least once every 2 or 3 days, with feeding frequency growing less as the spider matures. On the other hand, there are some keepers who "power feed" their tarantulas in the hopes that doing so might make them grow faster. This is done by feeding more frequently and increasing the habitat's temperature to increase the tarantula's metabolism. Others don't agree with this because they feel that it is unhealthy to force the tarantula's growth. There are no hard and fast rules regarding this, so it is really up to you.

As a general rule, a good feeding average is every 4-7 days for young spiders, and every 10-14 days for adults. This is variable, however, depending on the size of the food item you provide them. If you feed them larger insects, then you may not have to feed as frequently as you should when you are feeding smaller or medium-sized insects. Again, use your best judgment regarding this, and if in doubt – consult with those that have experience in feeding tarantulas of the same species that you are keeping. Different species do have different rates of growth.

If you notice them eating more and then suddenly stopping, it could mean that they are nearing their molt. Tarantulas fasting for a month or two before a molt is not unusual. They will not eat while molting, and feeding them for several days to about two weeks after a molt is recommended.

Most tarantulas are nocturnal, so many keepers prefer to feed their tarantulas at night, right before they go to bed. If they wake up in the morning and the food hasn't been eaten, they simply remove the food item from the cage. Again, if your tarantula doesn't feed, this is no cause for alarm. Simply wait another week or two, drop in another food item, and wait to see if the tarantula bites. You can keep repeating this on a weekly basis until your tarantula eats, or until your tarantula begins to molt, in which case you should wait until a few days to a week or more before once more attempting to feed them. Again, tarantulas that are molting are very vulnerable, and nothing can be worse than dropping in live prey into their enclosure when your tarantula is essentially weak and defenseless.

And finally, and again, remember to replenish your tarantula's water dish daily with clean and fresh drinking water to keep it from becoming dehydrated.

Chapter Seven: Tarantula Handling and Temperament

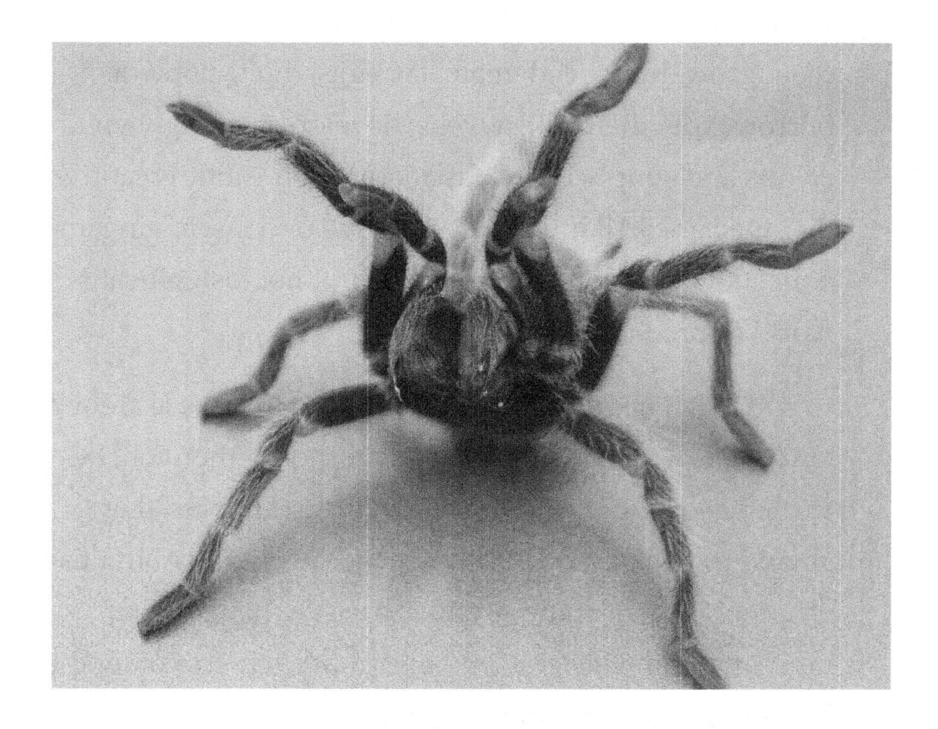

There is a reason why tarantulas have never been considered as mainstream pets – they are not "pets" in the traditional sense as most people understand it. They are dangerous, they will never show you affection, you can never cuddle with them, and it is not even advisable to handle them too much or too often. It can be said that tarantulas are pets that you can only look at and observe.

For hobbyists and keepers, however, this is satisfaction enough.

And there is certainly much to observe through those plastic or glass walls of their enclosure. A person can watch them grow, hunt, feed, mate, lay eggs, molt, climb or burrow, spin their silken webs, develop amazingly vivid colors, and simply be the fascinating and exotic creatures that they are. All in all, they can give us a fascinating and educational journey into the small but not insignificant world of predatory spiders.

Still, one must always remember that these are wild creatures, deserving of respect, and should therefore be treated accordingly. Not being mainstream pets, they should not be treated like most other pets, either. In this chapter, we give you tips on how best to handle your tarantula, some insights into a tarantula's behavior, and how best to minimize accidents in your ownership of a pet tarantula.

Tarantula Temperament

Each tarantula is different, and so is each species of tarantula. That is why it cannot be emphasized enough that you should do your research well beforehand. Larger tarantulas, some even measuring as long as a foot across, and these are the types that are extremely aggressive, extremely dangerous, and completely unsuitable to be made into pets. On the other hand, certain tarantulas are more docile than others, and these less aggressive species are recommended for beginners. But even with these "beginner" species, one can never be too careful in dealing with such a dangerous and lethal creature.

Tarantulas can be aggressive, or they can go on the defensive when they feel threatened. Most tarantulas have two main lines of defense: a venomous bite, and urticating hairs.

Many of the more docile species are skittish by nature, and they will prefer to run rather than bite. When they do bite, their venom is not usually enough to kill. Some have compared their venom to that of a bee sting. Still, for those who suffer an allergic reaction to those bites, it can potentially be fatal. If you are bitten and feel like you are having an allergic reaction, treat it as you would any other allergic reaction. Seek medical assistance immediately.

More commonly utilized by most tarantulas are a mechanical/chemical defense mechanism that involves their flicking of the urticating hairs on their abdomen. These are not actually hairs but skin extensions that the tarantula can launch at a threat by rubbing its legs against its abdomen, producing a cloud of "hairs" that contain tiny barbs that could potentially cause irritation or hives. The barbs attach to the victim and releases a toxin – many keepers have once or twice had to deal with urticating hairs that got into their eyes or nose. That bald spot in the middle of your tarantula's abdomen is a sign that it has been using its urticating hairs quite liberally.

Even if your tarantula has never shot its urticating hairs directly at you, be aware that tarantulas usually use these hairs around their burrow, weave them into their webs and egg sacs, and elsewhere around their cages. This is why it is prudent to proceed cautiously when dealing with tarantulas, or even when cleaning their cages. If you do become affected by the irritants in those hairs, cortisone cream can help relieve itching. But if you are experiencing any severe reaction, whether to a tarantula bite or to the toxins in their urticating hairs, it is always best to go directly to your doctor.

Tips for Handling Tarantulas

There is always a certain measure of risk that comes with handling tarantulas. So the very first question you should probably ask yourself is why do you want to do it? Most keepers and hobbyists recommend against too much handling of tarantulas – not only do you run the mild risk of being bitten or having urticating hairs flicked at you, you also run the risk of your tarantula escaping, being injured by a fall, or simply experiencing the stress of being handled when it may prefer to simply be left alone.

You may never need to actually handle your tarantula by hand. Even when you are moving your tarantula to a temporary container in order to clean out their cage, this can be done quite efficiently by prodding them with a brush and a cup. Some advocate learning how to handle your tarantula, while others feel it is unsafe and completely unnecessary. Whether you need to or want to, always use caution and safe practices in handling this beautiful but wild and potentially dangerous creature. In all cases, use your best judgment, and if you feel that the tarantula will not be tolerant of being handled, always err on the side of caution.

- Always move calmly and slowly – too much or too fast movement can startle your tarantula or put it immediately on the defensive/offensive.
- To pick up a tarantula, hold it between its second and third pair of legs using your thumb and forefinger. Or you can gently nudge it into the palm of your hand – this is called free handling a tarantula.
- Try to keep it in your hand as much as possible – don't allow it to crawl over the rest of your body or elsewhere. Always use both hands. This is for both you and your spider's safety. Always handle it above

a tall surface such as a table, with never more than 12 inches below. A fall is potentially dangerous for a tarantula as it can result in their abdomen rupturing or bursting and resulting in their death.

- Spiders do give warnings before they actually attack: a pose wherein the spider rears up on its back legs and then shows its fangs. Use common sense – if you see your tarantula adopting such a pose, don't even come near it. Just leave it alone.
- Keep it mind that a tarantula will never get "used" to handling; they will simply learn to tolerate it. But tarantulas are also unpredictable, and their mood and temperament can change often – sometimes on a daily basis. If you are going to handle a tarantula, you should first be familiar with its body signals and whether or not it appears like it will be tolerant in each particular moment. Their defensive/offensive movements are often simply instinctual, a conditioned response to perceived threats that is the result of millions of years of evolution. Be smart about it, and don't handle your tarantula if the tarantula does not look like it wants to be handled.

Behavioral Characteristics of Tarantulas

There are certain life changes common to all tarantulas that do, to a great extent, determine their behavior. While temperament-wise, each species is unique, and each individual spider even more so, some generalizations can at least be made regarding their behavior when threatened, feeding, during molting, and when a male reaches sexual maturity, among others.

Defensive Mechanisms

While film and media have variously portrayed tarantulas to be frightening, aggressive creatures, the truth is that many of them rarely bite, and would prefer to run when threatened. This does not mean they cannot be aggressive, because they certainly are – but only in response to a provocation, or a perceived threat. When provoked and are unable to escape, chances are good that they will bite. While tarantula bites have been compared to a bee sting, it can be a cause for concern for those who are highly allergic to tarantula venom.

When threatened, a defensive posture that a tarantula can adopt is to raise its two front pairs of legs in the air. This gives off the impression that they are larger than they actually are. And rather than biting, many will prefer to kick off their urticating hairs instead. These barbed hairs that contain toxins may seem feeble compared to venom, but they can become a cause of concern. Many keepers have had to suffer from the severe irritation of these hairs getting into their eyes or nose, and it is never a fun thing. If one's reaction is severe, emergency medical attention is recommended.

Feeding

Tarantulas use a variety of predatory moves in order to feed. Many tarantulas will first ambush their prey, paralyze it with venom, and then crush it with their fangs and jaws. Afterwards, they inject digestive enzymes into the prey in order to liquefy its body, and then proceed to feed by sucking up the liquefied prey through straw-like mouths.

Tarantulas don't eat their prey so much as they drink them – and some might think that those vampire-like fangs were no accident. In any case, this means that tarantulas get most of their moisture from their prey, and that there will always be a left-over carcass after a tarantula has finished feeding. These prey remnants should be cleaned out of the tarantula's enclosure regularly – not only do these become breeding ground for molds and fungus, leaving the carcass there for an undue length of time will only cause stress to your spider.

Spinning Silk

Unlike most spiders, tarantulas do not spin webs. They do spin silk, and their silk serves several purposes – to line their burrows, to act as a trip wire by which they can be alerted to the presence of prey. In this way, their silk serves several purposes: to protect their burrow, to provide them a more secure (and likely comfortable) retreat, and to help the tarantula in their hunt for and capture for prey.

Molting

Tarantulas periodically undergo molting, whereby they shed their old exoskeleton in order to grow. During this time, a tarantula can regrow lost limbs, and even replace internal organs.

A tarantula's exoskeleton will not expand with its growth, and so it will molt, It will shed its old exoskeleton – and this includes everything – from the lining of their outer skin to even the lining of their internal organs. You will notice a tarantula getting ready to molt when it stops eating, its color darkens, and becomes less active. Some species will spin quite a bit of silk prior to molting.

The period of molting is extremely stressful to a tarantula, and during this time, they should not be disturbed, nor should they be offered food – particularly live food.

Sexual Maturity among Males

Males become sexually mature once they reach their final molt, after which they will be seized by the drive to reproduce. You will find them spinning a specialized web where they can deposit sperm, and from which they will load up their pedipalps with sperm. When ready, they will go in search of a female.

It is not unusual to find the males consumed by this need to reproduce for the rest of its remaining life. It will typically spin their webs daily and copulate as many times as it can find a receptive female – until eventually they stop. Rather unfortunately, if they are not eaten or attacked by the female after mating, chances are that they will die soon afterwards. This is why males of most tarantula species usually have shorter lifespans compared to the females.

Chapter Eight: Breeding Your Tarantula

The reproduction and breeding of tarantulas is not like the breeding of mammals – the requirements are different, and are not quite as simple as putting a male and female together and hoping that little baby spiders are the result. Most times, putting two spiders together may actually result in a lot of fighting, or even cannibalism, and two adult injured spiders instead of tiny little spiderlings.

But before you even consider breeding from your tarantula, you should first ask yourself whether or not you should. As with most pets, breeding is not a decision that should be taken lightly, or on a whim. First of all, do your research beforehand to know what exactly is involved in the breeding of a spider and what it means to care for, nurture and raise young spiders. Then ask yourself what you are going to do with the young ones. Are you breeding your tarantulas for profit? While tarantulas are becoming more popular as exotic pets, that does not necessarily mean that a lot of people want them, or that there are enough people who will want to purchase any of the spiders you bred. Would you be willing to care for those spiders until they also grow into adults? Or are you simply planning on unloading them on a pet shop regardless of whether or not they are bought? Please remember that it is never advisable – and even illegal in some regions - to release foreign or non-native species into local ecology. You never know what havoc they might cause to the local wildlife, not to mention the human population.

Done right, however, and with the proper preparation and information, breeding your tarantula can be one of the most rewarding aspects of tarantula keeping. There is also the added bonus of less tarantulas being caught in the wild the more captive bred spiders are made available to keepers and hobbyists. The breeding process is also a great way to learn more about these fascinating and unique spiders – and success in this challenging endeavor helps ensure the ongoing viability of any tarantula species. And raising spiderlings – watching them grow from something so small and fragile to the hardy and colorful adults they eventually grow to be can be an amazing experience.

Learning Basic Tarantula Breeding Information

When a male spider reaches maturity, it will begin to weave a web mat onto which it will deposit its sperm. Using its pedipalps (short appendages between its chelicerae and front legs) into the pool of semen. The pedipalps absorb this semen and keeps it viable until a mate is found.

The male will actively look for a female, and may wander a bit until he finds her. The mating usually takes place near the female's burrow or shelter. When they meet, they will exchange signals that will both establish that they are of the same species, and also lull the female into being receptive of mating. Mating itself can be quite dangerous to the smaller male, and he uses small hooks on his legs called the tibial spurs to keep the female's jaws away from him. He will lift her up in order to gain access to her epigynum (genitals) which are located in her abdomen. Then he inserts his pedipalps into the female's opisthosoma, which is an opening in the lower surface of the female's abdomen. The semen is transferred into the female's body when the male deposits the sperm into the spermatheca, or sperm storage, until they are used to fertilize her eggs. After mating, the male will quickly leave the female's territory to avoid being killed or eaten, as females can often become aggressive afterwards.

Reproduction results from the joining of the sperm and the egg. In the wild, the female usually waits until spring when she spins a special web and deposits her eggs onto it, before she introduces the sperm that she had been storing. In this way, fertilization occurs. The female then wraps the eggs in a sac and she carries it with her via her fangs until the eggs are ready to hatch some 1-3 months later. The female will be quite aggressive during this time, and she will also turn the sac often to keep the eggs from deforming due to sitting too long. When the eggs finally do hatch, the young spiderlings will remain in their eggs for a time where they will live off of the yolk sac until they are ready to disperse. On the average, a female tarantula can lay anywhere between 50 to 2,000 viable eggs – yet another reason to consider carefully before actually breeding your pet tarantula.

Sexing Tarantulas

You will need a sexually mature male and female in order to successfully breed your tarantula, and they need to be of the same species. Please remember that crossbreeding is generally frowned upon in the industry. Not only will rehoming your hybrid spiderlings be challenging (if not impossible), but you are also removing the value of predictability in breeding potentially dangerous spiders. Even if you are successful in crossbreeding two different tarantula species (which may not always work), chances are good that the tiny spiders will not live long, or will not survive beyond the first generation (crossbreeds are usually sterile). Besides which, there are already more than 850 species of tarantula species in the world – if what you are looking for is more variety, there are literally hundreds to choose from without the spawning of a new and unpredictable crossbreed species.

Sexing tarantulas can be a confusing prospect – and even experts throughout the years have mistakenly pronounced one specimen to be male/female only later on to be proven wrong by an unmistakable female/male. What oftentimes may seem like obvious physical characteristics are not often reliable – to say that females are generally larger, and with wider abdomen than males, or that males are smaller and leggier than the females, is not a reliable way of sexing a tarantula unless you have other tarantulas to compare it to, or unless you are dealing with a mature male that is simply generally larger than the average. Some species do differentiate between male and female in terms of their coloring as mature adults, but for this you will have to wait for some time before being able to reliably distinguish the two sexes, and is not particularly useful if you are preparing or preselecting specimens for breeding. Nor is this reliable among species that do not differentiate between the sexes in terms of coloring.

That said, there are certain methods which, taken together, can help to confirm whether or not your tarantula is a male or a female. The first is the development of the tibial hooks on the male after his last molting – which means that he has reached sexual maturity and is now ready for reproduction. Underneath the first or front legs, you will find these tibial spurs, which are the "mating hooks" that the male uses to hold the female's fangs during mating. By this time, he will also have developed his sexual organs called the palpal bulb (embolus), also sometimes called "boxing gloves," at the end of his pedipalps. This is what he uses to transfer the sperm to the female during mating. If you find these two (the embolus and the tibial spurs), you are dealing with a sexually mature male. It bears mentioning, however, that not all species will have tibial hooks as mature males, so this is not necessarily a reliable method of sexing.

Another way of sexing a tarantula (and at an earlier period in a tarantula's life) is by examining their discarded exoskeleton. Microscopic examination of the tarantula's molted skin (exuvium), particularly within the abdominal portion, may reveal the spermathecae lining in which a female tarantula stores the sperm prior to fertilization. In some larger specimens, this is visible to the naked eye.

A more recent method (and one that has been called more reliable) of sexing live tarantula specimens is by examination of the epigastric furrow and the epiandrous fussilae. Males will be found to have additional spinnerets connected to the usual silk-producing epiandrous glands, and this is what they use in the production of the sperm web. This is an exciting method of sexing tarantulas because this can be done even before the tarantula is sexually mature, prior to molting, and has proven extremely reliable. That said, this and all the other methods of sexing tarantulas still does require some practice and plenty of knowledge about tarantula anatomy before one can get it right.

Tips for Breeding Tarantulas

Before you even contemplate breeding your tarantula, you need to have a plan on how to deal with what would most likely be hundreds of spiderlings. Soon after hatching from their eggs, you will need to house them individually, and then figure out a way to either care for them or distribute them. Establish contacts early on – who can you sell spiderlings to – wholesale dealership is highly recommended because caring for each spiderling individually until you can sell them to individual hobbyists can get overwhelming after some time, and you may not be able to care well for all your new spiders.

Breeding tarantulas begins after the male's last molting. Feed your male well for some two weeks after his final molt, and then you will notice him beginning to spin a small but thick band of silk. He will deposit the sperm onto this web and then using his palpal bulbs or secondary sex organs, he will begin the process of sperm induction in which he loads the emboli or palpal bulbs with sperm. When ready, he will dismantle this web and then go in search of a female.

Males will generally spin several webs throughout the rest of his remaining life, so you should make sure that he is not disturbed, and that he has sufficient room in his cage or enclosure to do this. In general, males will spin sperm webs each day until eventually, no webs are spun and the male dies of old age.

The female should also have recently molted and been allowed a few weeks to recover, during which she should be fed as much as she will take. Breeding should not take place any longer than six months after molting because after she passes this mark, the sperm stored in the spermathecae may be shed along with the old skin, given the time she will need for egg production. Wait until she recovers sufficiently from her final molt, and then you can introduce her to the male.

Tarantula courtship consists of the male vibrating his body and tapping his palps in the ground, alerting the female to his presence. If receptive, she will respond by drumming rapidly with her legs on the ground. Breeding takes place by the male securing the female's fangs with his tibial spurs, and then lifting the female to expose her underside. The male will insert his palps into the female epigynum in order to inject his sperm. When finished, he will release the female and retreat quickly when he feels it is safe to do so, during which time you should remove the male in order to prevent an attack from the female. In order to ensure a successful breeding, some keepers allow the males to spin another sperm web and then encourage another mating the next day.

The time between mating and egg laying varies between species, and can vary from a few weeks to several months. External factors such as feeding and temperatures can also affect the time of egg laying. Feed the female as much as she wants during this time. When she is ready, the female will start digging and begin to lay a silk nest. Many recommend providing her with a shelter during this time. The female will spin a very dense mat of thick silk onto which she will deposit the eggs, and then she will gather the silk together to create a kind of round ball. Other species will spin a type of fixed egg sac that cannot be moved around.

What follows is the incubation period during which time the female will be very protective of her eggs – turning or rotating them occasionally, guarding the eggs protectively, and rarely leaving it alone. Try not to disturb the female during this time. She will not want to feed during the incubation period, but clean and fresh water should still be offered her. Make sure that the cage is kept at optimal temperatures and humidity levels.

After several months, the spiderlings will begin to emerge. At first, they will be noticeable only in their nymph stage, but after a few days, they will undergo their first molt and then begin to look more like spiders. Leave them with their mother for several days to a few weeks, and then eventually you should remove the mother and the spiderlings should also be separated into individual pots or containers. You can begin to offer them suitable food such as fruit flies after a few days.

Raising Tarantula Spiderlings

With a leg span of about 0.25 – 0.5 inches (6-13 mm), Tarantula spiderlings, or "slings," as they are sometimes called, can seem very fragile and the novice breeder can feel more than a bit anxious about their care. For a novice breeder, caring for the slings can seem a bit overwhelming given the sheer number of all the hatched spiderlings – tarantulas can have a very large number of young. What is important is to do as much research as you could about the slings of the particular species you are breeding before you even begin to breed – make sure you have the correct set up, enclosures, etc., because their care can contrast markedly with the care of the adults of the species. It is best to contact or network with keepers who have managed to raise slings of your specific tarantula species and have a conversation regarding their real-life experience about raising and caring for tarantula spiderlings.

This section attempts to bring together some general guidelines on how to raise and care for tarantula slings, but you are encouraged to gather more information on your own, especially those pertaining to the particular species you are keeping and raising.

- Keep them in separate enclosures with ventilation that are not big enough for the tiny spiderlings to go through. Your best bet is to recycle old plastic jars with holes poked at the top using a needle or thumb tack. You will not be able to stack them (a problem if you are dealing with several hundred slings), so you will notice some horizontal space in which you can store your makeshift sling jars. Try to make sure that the holes you make for ventilation are not larger than the spiderling's carapace. Baby tarantulas are notorious escape artists, and you need to make sure that they will not slip through when you are not watching. Otherwise, goodbye baby tarantula.

- Another option is to seal up the lid with a wad of sterile cotton or foam that allows air circulation while effectively sealing up the ventilation holes against escaping spiderlings.
- Set up the enclosure with the necessary equipment: fill it halfway with substrate, a very low water dish (think small bottle caps), a tree bark or something similar to serve as a hiding place, and a few low plants. Make sure that the enclosure is sufficiently ventilated, while secure enough that the small sling will not be able to escape. You may wish to include some sphagnum moss as this can help maintain moisture or humidity inside the cage.
- Be very careful in moving your spiderling to its new enclosure. They look, and actually are, very fragile at this point. Move slowly, as quick movements can

startle them, and you don't want them bolting at the first opportunity. Place the entire container (usually it's a small sealed cylinder with rolled paper towels or tissue inside) on the substrate. Very carefully, using tweezers or tongs, extract the tissue or lining from the cylinder and begin to carefully unroll it. You may use a brush to encourage the sling off the towel. In no case should you handle the spiderling physically or by hand. Otherwise, you can simply open the vial or cylinder and leave it on the surface of the substrate until the sling comes out on its own.

- If you are breeding an arboreal or tree dwelling tarantula species, you will want to provide them with some climbing room. This can easily be done by decreasing the substrate level to less than half the container, and then providing the sling with a climbing surface – maybe a small piece of bark or a small sprig of plant. You may be pleasantly surprised to see your sling eventually creating its own retreat at the top of the plant or bark. Needless to say, you will not have to provide them with a burrow.
- Wait for a couple of days to let your sling acclimatize in its new environment before feeding it. You can, however, try feeding them the same day. Some slings will be hungry enough to eat right away.
- Keep their enclosure properly hydrated. Slings have not yet developed the waxy coating on their carapace

which can keep them from dehydrating, so they are more at risk of dehydration at this stage. This is true even for species that are native to dry or arid desert areas. Use tiny water dishes or even misting or spraying to ensure humidity.

- While spiderlings do require moist substrate – it can also be dangerous to make the substrate too moist. If the enclosure is excessively damp, spiderlings can die, so it is best to err on the side of dryness while you are attempting to find the perfect humidity levels for your little one. A dry substrate can quickly be re-moistened, but too wet substrate will take too long to dry out, which could be fatal to the spiderling in the meantime. This is true even for species that live in moist conditions or humid rainforests.
- As to temperatures, be sure to do species-specific research on which temperatures are optimal for your particular slings. Some do fine at room temperatures, while others prefer to keep theirs at slightly warmer temperatures as this could encourage faster growth. It should be noted that lower temperatures may encourage slower growth rates and lower appetites, even fasting in certain spiderlings. In general, between 68-75 F is a good range within which to keep slings.
- A sling's diet can consist of various insects – flightless fruit flies are a popular option for very small

tarantula spiderlings, or some other insect that is not bigger or longer than the spiderling's body. If you can't find live prey that is small enough, and are worried that live prey might end up attacking your sling, you can simply pre-kill the prey and drop it into the enclosure. This works because spiderlings are scavenge feeders in the wild, or they eat off larger prey that was killed by something else. Many spiderlings will do this quite well even in captivity. A cricket leg, for instance, will do to feed a single spiderling quite nicely. As a general rule, only provide them with food that is approximately the same length as the spiderling's body (including their legs). Some can be very aggressive feeders and will tackle too big prey or food to their own detriment.

- You can feed them well at a general average of about 2-3 times per week, but some keepers opt for "power feeding" in order to encourage maximum growth as much as possible. 2-3 times feeding per week is, however, already a pretty good average, and many normal growth spiderlings will quickly grow on this rate of feeding. You don't want to rush your spiderling, but you will certainly want it to grow as quickly as possible so that they will grow out of their delicate stage as quickly as possible.
- Clean out the spiderling's cage by removing boluses (the remnants of your spiderling's last meal) in order

to prevent the growth of bacteria or molds. Replace the water in their dish at least once each day. Once your spiderling has begun molting, you will also want to remove the old molt from the cage.

- The molting process in a young tarantula happens more frequently because of their quick growth. At first, you might find them molting at least once every month or every two months. A quick way to tell when they are preparing to molt is their sudden fasting – you should check on their food every day and remove any uneaten food to prevent the spiderling being attacked by its own food during the vulnerable molting time. If you notice your spiderling's coloration becoming duller, and its abdomen darker, it can mean that your sling is getting ready to molt. You should stop offering them food at this time. After molting, you should wait a few days before offering them food again. Wait until the sling's exoskeleton begins to harden – in the meantime, it should be left alone as much as possible. Remember to remove the exuvium immediately after the sling has finished molting.
- Once the spiderling begins to grow, you can begin to transfer them to a slightly larger, but similarly equipped, container. While it is advisable to refrain from handling the fragile spiderlings too much, when it is necessary, you should not handle them with your

bare hands. A brush with soft bristles (for instance, an artist's brush) is ideal, and gently brushing the spider to get them to move is the best method of manipulating the spiderling. Using a brush is generally safe, and many have noted that it seems to calm the spider rather than aggravate it.

- Finally, be patient – especially when dealing with newly hatched slings that may be hard to see against the substrate, or if the sling has preferred to hide itself by burrowing or hiding. You may find yourself cleaning out uneaten food for several days. It may often feel like all you're looking at is a tub of dirt and you wonder if your sling is still alive somewhere. Be patient – and be consistent in providing them the proper environment, diet and care. You may soon be rewarded with a darker colored, and visibly larger spiderling. It usually takes at least three years before a spiderling begins to look more like a slightly smaller version of its parents, with slightly different colors. Afterwards, they can be treated much as you would treat an adult tarantula.

Chapter Nine: Keeping Your Tarantula Healthy

It's always best to keep your tarantula in optimal health through appropriate living conditions and proper diet and nutrition. This is because it is not as easy to find veterinary care for tarantulas and other exotic pets as it is for most mainstream pets. You might find yourself having to travel quite a distance just to find a vet with enough experience, and willing to look at, your venomous and exotic pet. Some other options you may have, however, are locating an experienced tarantula owner, keeper or enthusiast with enough experience with ill tarantulas, or perhaps professional arachnid keepers that work within or in cooperation with a zoo or private collections.

The good news is that tarantulas are fairly hardy creatures. They can self-regulate their health, and provided they are kept in optimal conditions, the chances of you having to look for external professional intervention might not be too often or too likely.

Still, there are some common conditions that tarantulas can suffer from, and which it is advisable for you to be familiar with – not only to be able to identify these problems when they do crop up, but so that you have some familiarity with quick treatments or first aid interventions that you can act upon immediately.

Please always keep in mind that you are dealing with a potentially dangerous and even lethal creature – and they can become doubly more aggressive when they are injured or sick. Even the most laid back of species can be more likely to bite or attack defensively should you attempt to handle them while they are vulnerable.

A good rule of thumb is to wear protective gloves, to move slowly, and to handle them carefully. You might also want to place them in a cold container (for example, a refrigerator) for a short while before attempting to handle them because spiders generally become sluggish and lethargic when it is cold. This can help ensure the safety of both yourself and your pet.

Common Conditions Affecting Tarantulas

Some of the more common conditions that tarantulas can suffer from include:

- Dehydration
- Losing a leg
- Bleeding and injuries
- Bad molting
- Internal infection from mold and fungus
- Parasites

Dehydration

Dehydration is perhaps one of the most common conditions suffered by tarantulas in captivity. Even though you might never see your tarantula drinking, it is necessary to maintain the appropriate humidity levels in their enclosure – which you can do by providing them with a water dish that should contain clean and fresh water daily. Internally, they get most of their water intake from their food, but external humidity is just as essential to keep them from becoming dehydrated - and this is true even for desert tarantulas. Tarantulas that come from desert areas or regions generally live in burrows with higher humidity levels compared to the external environment. Aside from providing them with a water dish, you may occasionally want to spray the substrate in the tank to help maintain humidity.

One sign that your tarantula is becoming dehydrated is if you find it standing or hovering over its water dish. This means that it may be attempting to hydrate itself by standing over the water. If you find them doing this successively over several days, it can mean that there isn't enough humidity in their enclosure. When they really need to, you might just actually find them drinking water. This means that the spider is extremely dehydrated, and needs immediate "treatment."

Other signs and symptoms of dehydration include shrinking of the size and shape of the abdomen, and a gradual change to a hunched-up appearance with the legs curled underneath its body. In a general sense, your tarantula looks shriveled and sunken. You might also notice it becoming less active and more lethargic.

Needless to say, you need to address the humidity levels in your spider's enclosure immediately. While they can live for some time without food, they will certainly die without water. You will need to rehydrate your spider before its condition worsens, and you can do this by using a small plastic tub filled with water-soaked paper towels. Make sure that the lid has holes for sufficient ventilation. Place your spider on top of the paper towels and close the lid. Leave it for some time, in an area that is warm but not too hot so that the water can slowly evaporate. You'll probably notice significant improvement in your tarantula within the next 24 hours. Keepers and hobbyists refer variously to this treatment method as the "ICU" cup or the tarantula humidifier.

Losing a leg

Yes, eight legs (called pedipalps) may seem like a lot to start with, but losing one of them is no small thing. Unfortunately, any injury or accident suffered by your tarantula could potentially result in the loss of one or more of its eight limbs.

Should this happen, the good news is that your tarantula could eventually regenerate its missing limb. Wait for the next molt, and you might find that it has grown a new or replacement leg – though this is a bit smaller than the original one. It may take your pet another molting before it could recover a leg that looks more like the original.

The important thing is to make sure that your tarantula's injury heals cleanly. You can use skin adhesive to help staunch the bleeding of any wound, and then simply wait for your spider's natural process of recovery and regeneration during its invertebrate molting.

Bleeding and injuries

Various kinds of injuries can cause your tarantula to "bleed"- their blood being a kind of clear or yellowish liquid called "hemolymph. You don't want them losing a lot of their "blood," and so you will need to help staunch the wound.

Fortunately, this is not a complicated or difficult treatment to provide. All you need is a specialist skin adhesive glue, though superglue can work in emergencies. Just use it to repair the rupture or injury in their skin, and this can halt the flow of their yellowish "blood." This can even repair a severe rupture to the abdomen that may have resulted from a fall – provided treatment is provided quickly and immediately.

Keepers and hobbyists recommend always keeping superglue at hand, and consider it essential to your tarantula first aid kit. Of course, in this instance, prevention is always better than a cure, and it is recommended that you prevent any instance of an injury befalling your tarantula in the first place. If you are unsure of your tarantula's unique temperament, or especially if you know that your tarantula has a skittish character, minimize unnecessary handling in the first place to keep down incidences of injury. While the superglue treatment can seem to work wonders, don't forget that this might also cause your pet problems during their next molting – which in some cases can even result in their death. So take care that they don't get injured in the first place.

Bad molting

A bad molt happens when your tarantula could not get out of its old exoskeleton quickly enough before the old one hardens. The spider is then either trapped inside, or simply unable to separate itself from its old exoskeleton. This can happen if your spider is too old, too weak or malnourished, or too young. Sometimes, a difficulty in separating the old leg from the new leg can result in a deformed leg.

Making sure that your tarantula is healthy and well-hydrated should keep down the possibilities of a bad molt. If bad molting does happen, you can help them by using tweezers. Be very careful when you do this, however, because they are extremely fragile during this time. If you find your spider having trouble during his molting, you can help them by adding moisture or lubrication by using a wet paintbrush to make it easier for him to ease out of the old exoskeleton.

If the molting resulted in a deformed leg, you should wait until after the new exoskeleton has hardened (after at least four days), after which you can use tweezers to cleanly pluck off the deformed leg. This is really the best solution because if you leave the deformed leg until the next molting, your spider will again find itself facing molting difficulties. Meanwhile, care for your spider as best you can – feed it well and maintain its enclosure to bring it in good condition in time for the next molting.

Internal infection from mold and fungus

Internal infections can result from mold and fungus when you overdo the moisture and humidity in your tarantula's enclosure. Each species has its own temperature and humidity requirements, so it's best to do your research beforehand, and double check your information again. If there is too much moisture in their enclosure, fungus or molds can grow, and can cause infections to your tarantula's internal organs.

As with most illnesses, prevention is better than the cure – especially because this can be a potentially lethal condition for tarantulas to be in. You'll know that infection has set in when you notice uneven, cream-colored spots anywhere on your tarantula's body. You can try to give them treatment by moving them to a clean and well-ventilated housing and applying betadine to the infected areas. But when the infection has become large enough to be noticeable, it may often already be too late.

Parasites

Parasites are more common among the wild caught tarantulas as compared to the captive bred, though of course it can occur in either. Internal parasites can make your tarantula very ill, and sometimes unable to eat anything at all. One internal parasite common among tarantulas is the nematode, and a nematode invasion can manifest in various ways, such as spinning lots of silk, restlessness, refusal to eat, refusal to leave the water dish, a kind of sickly sweet odor, or a whitish mass near your spider's mouth. Unfortunately, there is still no effective treatment for nematode parasites.

Mites are another potential parasite that can affect tarantulas, and you can usually see them gathering around your spider's mouth. Use some petroleum jelly on a cotton swab and simply lift away the mites with the swab. The mites usually stick to the petroleum jelly and are easily lifted off.

Prevent any incidence of mites in the first place by providing sufficient ventilation and the right amount of humidity in your spider's enclosure. Clean and disinfect the terrarium and all its decorations and elements if mites or other parasites such as maggots or small flies have begun to settle inside the enclosure. Clean out the substratum regularly, including any waste and uneaten food – these can be perfect breeding grounds for bacteria and parasites.

A wild caught tarantula must never be mixed in the same enclosure as captive bred tarantulas at the risk of parasite transmission. Better yet, it is highly recommended that you purchase only captive bred rather than wild caught tarantulas in the first place.

Tarantula Care Sheet

To see a tarantula at a glance, or the nearest approximation of a quick acquaintance, is presented in this section. We present to you a quick summary of facts regarding tarantulas in general (keep in mind that variations will still prevail when it comes to each individual species). This condenses much of the information presented in this book, and offers the reader a comprehensive but detailed look at what caring for a tarantula could look like.

1.) Basic Tarantula Information

Kingdom: Animalia

Phylum: Arthropoda

Subphylum: Chelicerata

Class: Arachnida

Order: Araneae

Infraorder: Mygalomorphae

Family: Theraphosidae

Regions of Origin: United States, Central, South America, Africa, Asia, Australia, Spain, Portugal, Turkey, Italy, Cyprus

Primary Habitat: Varies depending on the species and region of origin, but can include savannahs, grasslands, rainforests, deserts, scrublands, mountains, and forest, in tropical and subtropical climates; they can either be terrestrial and burrowers in the ground, or arboreal and tree-dwelling

Description: Most are black or brown, but some species have more vivid coloring such as blue, orange, or yellow. They have 8 closely grouped eyes (2 large eyes surrounded by 3 eyes on each side; their bodies have two major parts –

the prosoma and the abdomen, that is connected by a pedicle which allows the two parts to move independently. Tarantulas, unlike true spiders, have fangs that point straight down instead of sideways. They have 8 legs, and their legs and abdomen are covered by thick hair.

Primary Behavioral Characteristics: Nocturnal, territorial, predatory, cannibalistic; can either be burrowers or arboreal

Health Conditions: Dehydration, Losing a leg, Bleeding and injuries, Bad molting, Internal infection from mold and fungus, Parasites

Lifespan: on the average, tarantulas can live up to 30 years

2.) Habitat Requirements

Recommended Equipment: 5 gallon tank or terrarium secured with a locking mesh screen top, and equipped with substrate, water dish, starter burrow and hide area

Recommended Temperature: 70-80 F

Cleaning Frequency: Spot cleaning daily, with a more thorough cleaning at least once every 4-6 months, or more frequently if necessary

3.) Feeding and Diet

Primary Diet: Crickets, grasshoppers, moths, cockroaches, mealworms, and other insects, with some adults also able to feed on pinkies and small lizards; in no case should the prey item exceed the size of the tarantula

Feeding Frequency (slings): Every 2-3 days

Feeding Frequency (juvenile): 1-2 times a week

Feeding Frequency (adult): depends on the species, the size of prey, the rate of growth

Water: Clean water in a water dish should be freely available

4.) Breeding Information

Age of Sexual Maturity: varies between species, can range from 2-5 years

Time of greatest fertility: within 6 months of an adult female's molting

Gestation Period: varies depending on species, temperature and feeding, but can range from 3-9 months

Incubation Period: varies, but can range from 6-9 weeks

Clutch Size: varies between species, but can range from 50-2,000

Size at Birth: 0.25 – 0.5 inches (6-13 mm)

Index

D

E

F

G

H

I

K

L

M

N

O

P

R

S

T

W

Y

Photo Credits

Page 1 Photo by Viki via Wikimedia Commons. <https://commons.wikimedia.org/wiki/File:Grammostola_cf._porteri_adult_male.jpg>

Page 5 Photo by Diro1962 via Pixabay. <https://pixabay.com/en/tarantula-spider-arachnophobia-1033341/>

Page 11 Photo by Buddy_Nath via Pixabay. <https://pixabay.com/en/spider-tarantula-hairy-arachnid-1232384/>

Page 21 Photo by Kapa65 via Pixabay. <https://pixabay.com/en/spider-tarantula-hairy-exotic-357185/>

Page 39 Photo by Rosado via Pixabay. <https://pixabay.com/en/arthropods-spider-tarantula-scary-1622783/>

Page 47 Photo by melly17 via Pixabay. <https://pixabay.com/en/spider-terrarium-tarantula-hairy-1170337/>

Page 55 Photo by HotelMonacoMuenchen via Pixabay. <https://pixabay.com/en/tarantula-brachypelma-spider-324917/>

Page 61 Photo by PaigeH via Pixabay. <https://pixabay.com/en/tarantula-spider-fuzzy-fangs-797095/>

Page 71 Photo by Dawson via Wikimedia Commons. <https://commons.wikimedia.org/wiki/File:Mating_rose_hair_tarantulas.jpg>

Page 89 Photo by andreasmetallerreni via Pixabay. <https://pixabay.com/en/tarantula-spider-macro-creepy-fear-336367/>

Page 99 Photo by BiKe2016 via Pixabay. <https://pixabay.com/en/poecilotheria-striata-tarantula-1198228/>

References

"Ailments & Treatments for Tarantulas." Pets on Mom.Me. <http://animals.mom.me/ailments-treatments-tarantulas-1283.html>

"Aphonopema seemanni." Wikipedia. <https://en.wikipedia.org/wiki/Aphonopelma_seemanni>

"Avicularia Versicolor/Pink Toe Tarantula." Tarantula Tarantulas. <http://www.tarantulapets.com/avicularia-versicolor-antilles-treespider-martinique-pink-toe/>

"Basic Tarantula Care."Michael Jacobi and TARANTULAS.com. <http://www.tarantulas.com/care_info.html>

"Basic Tarantula Care." TarantulaCages.com. <http://www.tarantulacages.com/tarantulacare.html>

"Beginner's Guide to the Brazilian Black Tarantula." Tarantula Heaven. <http://www.tarantulaheaven.com/beginners-guide-to-the-brazilian-black-tarantula/>

"Brachypelma albopilosum." Wikipedia. <https://en.wikipedia.org/wiki/Brachypelma_albopilosum>

"Brachypelma Albopilosum/Honduran Curly Hair." Tarantula Tarantulas.

<http://www.tarantulapets.com/brachypelma-albopilosum/>

"Brachypelma Emilia." Wikipedia. <https://en.wikipedia.org/wiki/Brachypelma_emilia>

"Brachypelma Smithi/Mexican Red Knee Tarantula." Tarantula Tarantulas. <http://www.tarantulapets.com/mexican-red-knee-tarantula-b-smithi/>

"Brazilian Black Tarantula (Grammostola Pulchra)." Gpulchra. <http://gpulchra.blogspot.com/p/care-and-housing.html>

"Breeding."giantspiders.com. <http://giantspiders.com/breeding/>

"Breeding Tarantulas."Mike's Basic Tarantula. <http://www.mikebasictarantula.com/Breeding.html>

"Bugs/Tarantula." Wikijunior. <https://en.wikibooks.org/wiki/Wikijunior:Bugs/Tarantula>

"Buying Tarantulas – Online Vendors."Cancerides. <https://tomsbigspiders.wordpress.com/2014/04/20/buying-tarantulas-online-vendors/>

"Cage & Habitat." Tarantula Guide. <http://www.tarantulaguide.com/pet-tarantula-cage-and-habitat/>

"Care Sheet Costa-Rican Zebra Tarantula (Aphonopelma seemanni)." Martin Overton. <http://arachnophiliac.com/burrow/caresheets/aphonopelma_semmanni.htm>

"Chaco Golden Knee Tarantula (Grammostola pulchripes)." Exotic Pets. <http://www.exotic-pets.co.uk/chaco-golden-knee-tarantula.html>

"Chilean Rose Tarantula." Wikipedia. <https://en.wikipedia.org/wiki/Chilean_rose_tarantula>

"Chilean Rose Tarantulas as Pets." Lianne McLeod, DVM. <http://exoticpets.about.com/cs/tarantulas/p/chileanrose.htm>

"Chromatopelma Cyaneopubescens/Green Bottle Blue Tarantula." Tarantula Tarantulas. <http://www.tarantulapets.com/chromatopelma-cyaneopubescens-greenbottle-blue/>

"Costa Rican Zebra Tarantula." Jon Fouskaris. <http://www.petbugs.com/caresheets/A-seemani.html>

"Costa Rican Zebra Tarantulas as Pets." Lianne McLeod, DVM. <http://exoticpets.about.com/cs/tarantulas/p/costaricanzebra.htm>

"Cross breeding." British Tarantula Society. <http://thebts.co.uk/forums/showthread.php?2828-Cross-breeding>

"Curly Hair Tarantulas (Brachypelma albopilosum) as Pets." Lianne McLeod, DVM. <http://exoticpets.about.com/cs/tarantulas/p/Curlyhairtaran.htm>

"Diseases." Mikhail F. Bagaturov. <http://tarantulas.su/en/diseases>

"Eupalaestrus campestratus." Mike's Basic Tarantula. <http://www.mikebasictarantula.com/Eup-campestratus-care-sheet.html>

"Eupalaestrus campestratus." Wikipedia. <https://en.wikipedia.org/wiki/Eupalaestrus_campestratus>

"Eupalaestrus Camestratus/Pink Zebra Beauty." Tarantula Tarantulas. <http://www.tarantulapets.com/eupalaestrus-campestratus-pink-zebra-beauty/>

"Food & Diet." Tarantula Guide." <http://www.tarantulaguide.com/tarantulas-food-water-diet/>

"Glossary." Tung. <http://tarantulakeeper.blogspot.com/2008/12/glossary.html>

"Grammostola pulchra."Mike's Basic Tarantula. <http://www.mikebasictarantula.com/Gram-pulchra-care-sheet.html>

"Grammostola pulchra."Wikipedia.
<https://en.wikipedia.org/wiki/Grammostola_pulchra>

"Grammostola pulchripes." Mike's Basic Tarantula.
<http://www.mikebasictarantula.com/Gram-pulchripes-care-sheet.html>

"Grammostola pulchripes." Wikipedia.
<https://en.wikipedia.org/wiki/Grammostola_pulchripes>

"Grammostola Pulchripes Care Sheet." AL.
<http://terrestrialtarantulas.blogspot.com/2011/01/chaco-golden-knee-caresheet-grammostola.html>

"Green Bottle Blue Tarantula." Tarantula Guide.
<http://www.tarantulaguide.com/tarantulas/green-bottle-blue-tarantula/>

"Greenbottle blue tarantula."Wikipedia.
<https://en.wikipedia.org/wiki/Greenbottle_blue_tarantula>

"Handling." Tarantula Guide.
<http://www.tarantulaguide.com/handling-pet-tarantulas/>

"Handling Tarantulas – Some Things to Consider." Cancerides.
<https://tomsbigspiders.wordpress.com/2014/11/26/handling-tarantulas-some-things-to-consider/>

"How do tarantulas reproduce?" Quora. <https://www.quora.com/How-do-tarantulas-reproduce>

"How to Make a Pet Tarantula Habitat You Can Be Proud Of." Kristine Lacoste. <http://www.petful.com/other-pets/how-make-pet-tarantula-habitat/>

"How to Recognize a Sick Tarantula." Hacked By ReFLeX. <http://www.tarantulaspider.net/how-to-recognize-a-sick-tarantula/>

"How do tarantulas reproduce?" Reference.com. <https://www.reference.com/pets-animals/tarantulas-reproduce-2a48896e08363835>

"How to Care for Tarantula Spiderlings." Hacked By ReFLeX. <http://www.tarantulaspider.net/how-to-care-for-tarantula-spiderlings/>

"How to Determine the Sex of Your Tarantula." Mark R. Hart. <http://www.birdspiders.com/faq_sex.php>

"How to Handle Tarantulas." Pet-Tarantulas.com. <http://www.pet-tarantulas.com/tarantulas/how-to-handle-tarantula.html>

"Is a Tarantula the Right Pet for You – the Pros & Cons." Bog Big. <http://bogbit.com/is-a-tarantula-the-right-pet-for-you-the-pros-cons/>

"Keeping Tarantulas as Pets." Dog Breed Info. <http://www.dogbreedinfo.com/pets/tarantula.htm>

"Keeping Tarantulas – The Basics." Richard C. Gallon. <http://www.thebts.co.uk/keeping_tarantulas.html>

"Methods for Sexing Tarantulas." Mile High Bug Club. <http://milehighbugclub.com/Methods%20for%20Sexing%20Tarantulas.htm>

"Mexican redknee tarantula." Wikipedia. <https://en.wikipedia.org/wiki/Mexican_redknee_tarantula>

"Mexican Redknee Tarantulas as Pets." Lianne McLeod, DVM. <http://exoticpets.about.com/cs/tarantulas/p/mexredknee.htm>

"Mexican Red Leg." Tarantula Guide. <http://www.tarantulaguide.com/tarantulas/mexican-red-leg-tarantula/>

"Mexican Redleg Tarantulas as Pets." Lianne McLeod, DVM. <http://exoticpets.about.com/cs/tarantulas/p/mexicanredleg.htm>

"Pet Ownership Costs." Pet Nutrition Info.com. <http://www.petnutritioninfo.com/cost-to-own-a-pet.html>

"Pet Tarantulas." Lianne McLeod, DVM. <http://exoticpets.about.com/cs/tarantulas/a/tarantulasaspet.htm>

"Pinktoe (avicularia)." Tarantula Heaven. <http://www.tarantulaheaven.com/pinktoe-avicularia/>

"Pinktoe Tarantula." Animal World. <http://animal-world.com/encyclo/reptiles/spiders/pinktoedtarantula.php>

"Pinktoe tarantula." Wikipedia. <https://en.wikipedia.org/wiki/Pinktoe_tarantula>

"Pros and cons of having a tarantula pet." Super User. <http://homeanimals.co.uk/30-pros-and-cons-of-having-tarantula-pet>

"Raising Young Tarantulas (aka "Spiderlings")."Michael Jacobi and TARANTULAS.com. <http://www.tarantulas.com/spiderlings.html>

"Rescued Tarantulas in need of homes…" BTS Community Board. <http://thebts.co.uk/forums/showthread.php?6022-Rescued-Tarantulas-in-need-of-homes>

"Sexing a Tarantula." Michael Jacobi and TARANTULAS.com. <http://www.tarantulas.com/sexing.html>

"Sexing Tarantulas Using Molts." Cancerides. <https://tomsbigspiders.wordpress.com/2015/11/08/sexing-tarantulas-using-molts/>

"Should You Consider Breeding From Your Tarantula?" pets4homes.co.uk. <http://www.pets4homes.co.uk/pet-

advice/should-you-consider-breeding-from-your-tarantula.html>

“So you want to keep… Tarantulas.” Carl Portman. <http://www.thebts.co.uk/so_you_want_to_keep.htm>

“Spiders as Pets.” Veterinarians.com. <http://www.veterinarians.com/articles/spiders-as-pets.html>

“Tarantula.” National Geographic. <http://animals.nationalgeographic.com/animals/bugs/tarantula/>

"Tarantula.” Online Etymology Dictionary. <http://www.etymonline.com/index.php?term=tarantula>

“Tarantula.” Wikipedia. <https://en.wikipedia.org/wiki/Tarantula>

“Tarantula Cages.” Tarantula Tarantulas. <http://www.tarantulapets.com/tarantula-cages/>

“Tarantula Facts.” Amazing Tarantulas. <http://www.amazingtarantulas.com/tarantulafacts.htm>

“Tarantula Facts.” Jessie Szalay. <http://www.livescience.com/39963-tarantula.html>

“Tarantula Feeding – What, when, and how much to feed.” Cancerides. <https://tomsbigspiders.wordpress.com/2015/02/02/tarantula-feeding-how-much-to-feed/>

"Tarantula First Aid." Tarantulas.com.
<http://www.tarantulas.com/first_aid.html>

"Tarantula Glossary." PJ.
<http://zj2008.blogspot.com/2009/02/tarantula-glossary.html>

"Tarantula Health and Wellness." Pets4Homes.co.uk.
<http://www.pets4homes.co.uk/pet-advice/tarantula-health-and-wellness.html>

"Tarantula Rescue." Arachnoboards.
<http://arachnoboards.com/threads/tarantula-rescue.71924/>

"Tarantula Sling Husbandry – A Comprehensive Guide." Tom's Big Spiders.
<https://tomsbigspiders.wordpress.com/tag/raising-tarantula-slings/>

"Tarantula Spider Facts, Identification & Control." Orkin International.
<http://www.orkin.com/other/spiders/tarantulas/>

"Tarantula Study." jrscience.
<http://jrscience.wcp.muohio.edu/nsprojects/ns1images/tarantulas/tarantulapage/spiderpaper.html>

"Tarantula Term Glossary." Arachnid Menagerie.
<http://arachnidmenagerie.blogspot.com/p/glossary.html>

“Tarantulas as Pets.” LLL Reptile. <https://www.lllreptile.com/articles/106-tarantulas-as-pets/>

“Tarantulas: Terrible or Terrific!” Cornell University. <https://blogs.cornell.edu/spiders/tarantulas-terrible-or-terrific/#species>

“The Greenbottle blue Tarantula (Chromatopelma cyaneopubescens).” Todd Gearhart. <http://arachnophiliac.com/burrow/caresheets/chromatopelma_cyaneopubescens.htm>

“The Needs & Habitat of the Chaco Golden Knee Tarantula.” Pets on Mom.Me. <http://animals.mom.me/needs-habitat-chaco-golden-knee-tarantula-5814.html>

“The Pros and Cons of Some of the Most Popular Exotic Pets for Kids.” Metro Parent/daily. <http://www.metroparent.com/daily/house-home/family-pet/the-pros-and-cons-of-some-of-the-most-popular-exotic-pets-for-kids/>

“What Do Tarantulas Eat?” Tarantula Tarantulas. <http://www.tarantulapets.com/what-do-tarantulas-eat/>

“Why is crossbreeding a taboo in the hobby?” Tarantula Forum. <http://www.tarantulaforum.com/threads/why-is-cross-breeding-is-a-taboo-in-the-hobby.4239/>

"Wildlife as Pets." Mass. Gov. Energy and Environmental Affairs. <http://www.mass.gov/eea/agencies/dfg/dfw/fish-wildlife-plants/wildlife-as-pets.html>

Feeding Baby
Cynthia Cherry
978-1941070000

Axolotl
Lolly Brown
978-0989658430

Dysautonomia, POTS Syndrome
Frederick Earlstein
978-0989658485

Degenerative Disc Disease Explained
Frederick Earlstein
978-0989658485

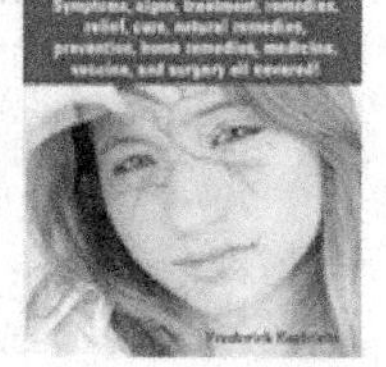

Sinusitis, Hay Fever,
Allergic Rhinitis Explained
Frederick Earlstein
978-1941070024

Wicca
Riley Star
978-1941070130

Zombie Apocalypse
Rex Cutty
978-1941070154

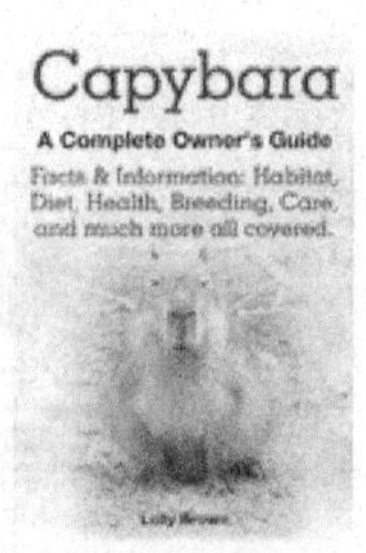

Capybara
Lolly Brown
978-1941070062

Eels As Pets
Lolly Brown
978-1941070167

Scabies and Lice Explained
Frederick Earlstein
978-1941070017

Saltwater Fish As Pets
Lolly Brown
978-0989658461

Torticollis Explained
Frederick Earlstein
978-1941070055

Kennel Cough
Lolly Brown
978-0989658409

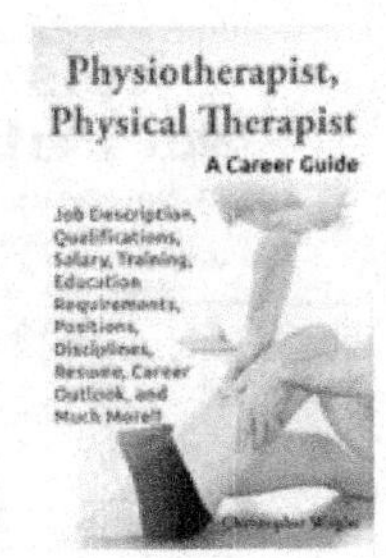

Physiotherapist, Physical Therapist
Christopher Wright
978-0989658492

Rats, Mice, and Dormice As Pets
Lolly Brown
978-1941070079

Wallaby and Wallaroo Care
Lolly Brown
978-1941070031

Bodybuilding Supplements
Explained
Jon Shelton
978-1941070239

Demonology
Riley Star
978-19401070314

Pigeon Racing
Lolly Brown
978-1941070307

Dwarf Hamster
Lolly Brown
978-1941070390

Cryptozoology
Rex Cutty
978-1941070406

Eye Strain
Frederick Earlstein
978-1941070369

Inez The Miniature Elephant
Asher Ray
978-1941070353

Vampire Apocalypse
Rex Cutty
978-1941070321